Hello, Family Members,

Learning to read is one of the most important accomplishments of early childhood. **Hello Reader!** books are designed to help children become skilled readers who like to read. Beginning readers learn to read by remembering frequently used words like "the," "is," and "and"; by using phonics skills to decode new words; and by interpreting picture and text clues. These books provide both the stories children enjoy and the structure they need to read fluently and independently. Here are suggestions for helping your child *before*, *during*, and *after* reading:

Before

- Look at the cover and pictures and have your child predict what the story is about.
- Read the story to your child.
- Encourage your child to chime in with familiar words and phrases.
- Echo read with your child by reading a line first and having your child read it after you do.

During

- Have your child think about a word he or she does not recognize right away. Provide hints such as "Let's see if we know the sounds" and "Have we read other words like this one?"
- Encourage your child to use phonics skills to sound out new words.
- Provide the word for your child when more assistance is needed so that he or she does not struggle and the experience of reading with you is a positive one.
- Encourage your child to have fun by reading with a lot of expression . . . like an actor!

After

- Have your child keep lists of interesting and favorite words.
- Encourage your child to read the books over and over again. Have him or her read to brothers, sisters, grandparents, and even teddy bears. Repeated readings develop confidence in young readers.
- Talk about the stories. Ask and answer questions. Share ideas about the funniest and most interesting characters and events in the stories.

I do hope that you and your child enjoy this book.

—Francie Alexander
  Reading Specialist,
  Scholastic's Learning Ventures

For BAT CONSERVATION INTERNATIONAL,
with admiration for their work
in saving the bats.
— M.B. and G.B.

Special thanks to Laurie Roulston
of the Denver Museum of Natural History
for her expertise

If you would like to learn more about bats, please contact:
Bat Conservation International
P.O. Box 162603, Austin, Texas 78716-2603
Telephone: (512) 327-9721   Fax: (512) 327-9724

Photography credits:
[Cover (bat in foreground): Benny Odeur-Wildlife Pictures/Peter Arnold, Inc.; (background): Merlin D. Tuttle/Bat Conservation International;] pages 1 and 29: Merlin D. Tuttle/Bat Conservation International; pages 3 and 37: Auscape (J-P Ferrero)/Peter Arnold, Inc.; pages 4-5: Karen Marks/Bat Conservation International; pages 6-7: Merlin D. Tuttle/Bat Conservation International; page 8: Robert and Linda Mitchell; pages 9-11: Merlin D. Tuttle/Bat Conservation International; pages 12-13: Robert and Linda Mitchell; page 14: Art Wolfe/Tony Stone Images; page 15: Tim Martin/BBC Natural History Unit; page 16-17: Merlin D. Tuttle/Bat Conservation International; pages 18-19: Albert Visage/Peter Arnold, Inc.; page 20: Roland Seitre/Peter Arnold, Inc.; page 21: Robert and Linda Mitchell; page 22: Merlin D. Tuttle/Photo Researchers, Inc.; pages 23-25: Merlin D. Tuttle/Bat Conservation International; page 26: Merlin D. Tuttle/Bat Conservation International/Photo Researchers, Inc.; page 27: Wolfgang Bayer/Bruce Coleman Inc.; page 28: Merlin D. Tuttle/Bat Conservation International/Photo Researchers, Inc.; pages 30-31: Merlin D. Tuttle/Bat Conservation International; page 32: Gunter Ziesler/Peter Arnold, Inc.; page 33: Rexford Lord/Photo Researchers, Inc.; page 34: Rob and Ann Simpson; page 36: Merlin D. Tuttle/Bat Conservation International; page 38: Roland Seitre/Peter Arnold, Inc.; page 40: Brian Keeley/Bat Conservation International.

Library of Congress Cataloging-in-Publication Data

Berger, Melvin.
    Screech! : a book about bats / by Melvin and Gilda Berger.
      p. cm. — (Hello reader! Science — Level 3)
    Summary: Simple text and photographs depict the physical characteristics, behavior, and habitats of different kinds of bats, as well as various myths about this flying mammal.
      ISBN: 0-439-20164-0 (pbk.)
      1. Bats—Juvenile literature. [1. Bats.] I. Berger, Gilda. II. Title. III. Series. IV. Hello science reader! Level 3.

QL737.C5 B43 2000
599.4—dc21

00-020050

12 11 10 9 8 7 6 5 4 3 2 1   00 01 02 03 04 05 06

Printed in the U.S.A.
First printing, August 2000

SCREECH!

A Book About Bats

by Melvin & Gilda Berger

Hello Reader! Science — Level 3

New Yo ney
M

CHAPTER ONE
Bats Alive

It's early one summer night.
You're taking a walk.
Something furry flits through the air
overhead.

Is it a bird?
No.
It has no feathers and no beak.

Is it a mouse?
No.
A mouse can't fly.

Is it a butterfly?
No.
It's bigger than a butterfly.

Then, what is it?
It's a bat!

Bats are mammals.
Cats and dogs, horses and cows,
lions and tigers — they're mammals,
too.
And so are human beings.

In many ways, bats are like other
mammals.
They grow inside their mother and are
born live.
They get milk from their mother's body.
They have hair or fur on their skin.

But in one way, bats are very different
from all other mammals.
They can fly!
Bats zip through the air faster than
you can blink an eye.

Most bats are born in June.
A mother bat usually has
only one baby at a time.
A baby bat is called a pup.

Some pups are born
with pink skin and no hair.
Their eyes are closed at birth.
Other pups have fur on their skin.
These pups start life with open eyes.

Huge numbers of mother bats give birth
at the same time.
The mothers and pups live together
in giant nurseries.
A single nursery may hold over a
million bats!

At first, the mother nurses her pup.
She feeds it milk from her body about
twice a day.

After each feeding, the mother leaves
the nursery.
She flies away to find food for herself.

When she returns, she goes to her baby.
Sometimes it is just where she left it.
But other times, it has moved somewhere
else.
How does the mother bat find her own
little pup?

Each baby bat has its own special chirp
and smell.
Every mother bat knows them very well!

By August, the pups are old enough to
hunt for themselves.

They fly out and join a colony of bats.

The colony may live in

- a large cave,
- an attic,
- a barn,
- or a garage.

Some bats make their homes in trees.

The homes of bats are called roosts.

Early each morning, the bats settle into their roosts.
They hook their claws into a wall or ceiling.
And they hang upside down!

The bats fold their wings around their bodies.
They lick their wings clean.
With their thumbs, they clean their faces.
They use the long, curved claws on their feet to groom themselves.
Then they fall asleep.

The bats sleep until it starts to get dark
outdoors.
Then they wake and fly out of the roost.
Sometimes millions of bats rise up
together.
They look like a cloud of thick smoke
against the sky.

At night, the bats hunt for food.
Most fly through the air catching insects.
Others eat fruit or flowers.
Some feed on fish or frogs.
A few drink blood.

By dawn, they're back home.
It's time to settle down.
Shhh. The bats are asleep.
Pleasant dreams!

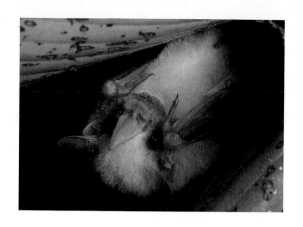

CHAPTER TWO
Bat Shapes and Sizes

You may think all bats look the same.
Well, they don't!
There are almost 1,000 different kinds
of bats.
Each has its own shape and size.

Some have a head shaped like a dog's
or a bear's head.
Others have a nearly flat face.
Many have an extra flap of skin
on their snout.
It's called a nose leaf.

Townsend's big-eared bat got its name for a good reason.
It has huge ears.
In fact, its ears are so long that the bat rolls them up when it goes to sleep!

Other bats have ears that are much smaller.
Take the ears of the **Rodrigues fruit bat**, for example.
They look like tiny tufts of hair.

A **Mexican free-tailed bat** has a long, thin tail.
A **tube-nosed fruit bat** has no tail at all.

The **hoary bat**'s fur is a spotty mixture of white and brown hairs.

The **red bat** has red fur with white tips.

All bats have a skeleton like yours.
They have arm and leg bones as you do.
They also have hand and foot bones.
But there is one big difference between
bats and humans.
A bat has super-long fingers.
A thin skin covers the arms and hands.
The bones and skin form the bat's wings.

A bat's body is perfect for flying.
Bats have light bones and small bodies.
This gives them less weight to carry
through the air.
And their big wings let them fly
with ease.
Some bats can fly as fast as
15 miles an hour!

The **flying fox** is the largest of all bats.
It weighs about two pounds.
Its body is the size of a pigeon's.
But its wings are nearly three times as
long as a pigeon's.
The distance from tip to tip is about
six feet!

The flying fox lives in warm, tropical
areas.
It is a fruit bat.
Fruit bats usually roost in treetops.
They like to eat ripe, squishy fruit best.
Sometimes they feed on flowers.

Fruit bats have very large eyes.
They can see better than
other bats.
Fruit bats use their eyes
and nose to find food.
Their ears are tiny.

The smallest bat
is the **Kitti's
hog-nosed bat**.
The size of a bee,
it weighs less
than a penny!
In fact, this bat
is among the
smallest of
all mammals.

A Kitti's hog-nosed bat also lives
where it is warm.
But this bat is an insect bat —
like most bats.
It eats bugs, not fruit.
Insect bats catch their
favorite food in midair.

How do insect bats find bugs?
The bats flit through the air making
high-pitched sounds.
Squeak — squeak — squeak.
The little screeches come quickly,
one after another.

Some bats squeak with their mouths.
Others squeak through their noses.
You can't hear the squeaks.
They are much too high
for human ears.

Sooner or later, the bat's squeaks hit
an insect.
The sounds bounce back.
It is like clapping in a tunnel.
Each clap makes an echo.

An insect bat has big ears.
They pick up the echoes.
Echoes that come back quickly mean the
insect is close.
Echoes that take longer mean the insect
is far away.

In a flash, the bat knows
- how far away the insect is,
- how fast it is traveling,
- which direction it is moving,
- and its size.

The bat zooms toward its prey.
ZAP!
It grabs the insect with its mouth.
Or it uses its wings to scoop up the bug.

Bats eat small insects right away.
The bats carry the large insects home.

Did you know that bats help humans?
Fruit bats help spread seeds around.

A fruit bat grabs a fruit from a tree.
As the bat flies away, it eats the fruit.
The seeds drop to the ground.
Some of the seeds sprout.
New plants start to grow.

Or, a fruit bat flicks its long tongue
into a flower.
The bat's tongue gets covered
with pollen.
Then the bat flies to another flower.
Some of the pollen rubs off.
This flower makes new seeds.
And the seeds grow into new plants.

The **greater short-nosed bat** is a good
example of a fruit bat.
It feeds on the pollen of wild banana
plants.
Without these bats, the plants would
die out.
Without the plants, the bats would
die out.
The bats and plants really need
each other!

Insect-eating bats help us, too.
Many insects are pests.
Pesty insects

- bite or sting people and animals,
- spread diseases,
- and destroy crops.

Bats gulp down huge numbers
of insect pests.

Some bats nab about 600 insects
an hour.
But the **gray bat** gets the prize.
Its nightly catch can be as large as
3,000 insects!

Fishing bats of Central and South America catch fish.
One fishing bat can eat as many as 40 small fish in a night!

The bat flies just above the surface of rivers and lakes.

It aims its squeaks down toward the water.

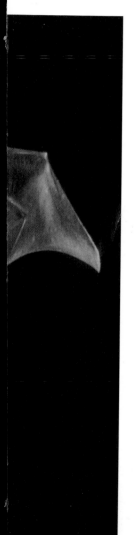

Suddenly, some echoes come back faster.

The bat senses a ripple in the water.

It's made by a fish swimming near the surface.

The bat drops its feet into the water.

It scoops up the fish with its big, sharp claws.

POP!

Into its mouth the fish goes.

Sometimes a fishing bat falls into the water.

That's no problem.

The bat swims to safety.

It uses its wings as oars!

Vampire bats are small bats.
They live only in Central and South America.
Vampire bats feed on blood.
They need the blood to live.
The blood mostly comes from cattle.

A vampire bat lands near a sleeping cow
or horse.
Silently, it creeps closer.
Soon, the bat is ready
to strike.

With its sharp teeth, it makes a tiny cut
in the animal's skin.
The cow or horse doesn't feel anything.
It doesn't even wake up.
Blood flows from the wound.
The bat doesn't suck the blood.
It just laps it up.

Once in a while, vampire bats may attack
a person who is asleep.
The bat heads for the toes.
A quick bite — a few licks — and away the
bat flies.
The person sleeps on.

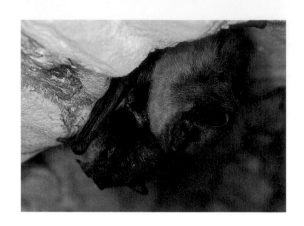

CHAPTER THREE
Bats Through the Year

In warm weather, bats have lots to eat.
Insect bats catch plenty of bugs.
Fruit bats feed on growing plants.

But warm weather doesn't always last.
In many places the days and nights
grow cold.
Snow may fall.

What do the bats do then?
What do they eat?
How do they keep warm?

Many bats hibernate (HYE-bur-nate)
for the winter.
They go into a very deep sleep.
The bats breathe very slowly.
Their hearts slow from 900 beats to
20 beats a minute.
And their body temperature drops
way down.

Bats hibernate in different places.
Barns or attics are common.
So are caves and hollow trees.
Millions of bats may end up in the
same place.
Some tuck themselves in snugly.
Others want plenty of room.

Hibernating bats look as if they are dead.
But they're not.
In spring, the hibernating bats wake up.
And away they fly.

Some other bats migrate (MYE-grate)
before it gets cold.
They head to warmer places.
Sometimes they fly for hundreds
of miles.

In time, the bats reach their winter
homes.
There they stay until the weather starts
to change.
Then the bats return to their old roosts.

Of course, some bats stay in one place
all year long.
They live where it is always warm.
These bats do not hibernate.
They do not migrate.
They have everything
they need just where
they are.

CHAPTER FOUR
Bats in Danger

Many people are afraid of bats.
They believe myths about bats.
They don't know the facts.

Myth: Bats get tangled in people's hair.
Fact: Bats' sharp senses stop them
from flying into people.

Myth: Bats are often sick and dirty.
Fact: Bats are very clean, and few carry diseases.

Myth: Bats bring bad luck.
Fact: Bats help people and the places where
they live.

Myth: Vampire bats attack humans.
Fact: Vampire bats feed mostly on cattle.

Sad to say, the number
of bats is going down.
Many kinds are in danger
of disappearing forever.
Can you guess why?

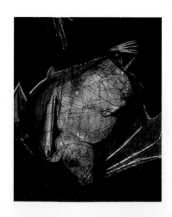

Myths give people false ideas about bats.
This leads them to hurt bats.

Most bats live in wild areas.
When people move in, they get rid of bats.
The people build roads and homes.
The bats have less and less food to eat.
Many starve to death.

People explore bat caves.
They drive out sleeping or
hibernating bats.
Other people fix up their attics.
They knock down old barns and garages.
Bats find fewer places to roost.
Without places to live, bats die.

In many tropical countries,
people hunt bats for food.
In the past, they killed them
with bows and arrows.

Today they use guns.
The hunters stretch nets
across caves where bats roost.
They catch and kill many more bats
than ever before.

Bats are in danger.
And so are we.
Fewer bats mean more insect pests.
Fewer bats also mean fewer new plants.

Bats need our help.
Get rid of the myths.
Tell everyone the facts about bats.
Help spread the word.